A Companion Anthology to Literature for Teaching

Solo Vocal Repertoire for Singers and Teachers of Singers

Soprano Edition

by
Christopher Arneson and Lauren Athey-Janka

Inside View Press

Solo Vocal Repertoire for Singers and Teachers of Singers
Soprano Edition

by

Christopher Arneson
&
Lauren Athey-Janka

ISBN: 978-0-9910876-3-1

Printed in the United States of America

Inside View Press
Gahanna, Ohio
www.VoxPed.com

Introduction

The intent of this book is to provide tools that will help students and teachers achieve their pedagogic goals. The repertoire we have chosen, along with the technical instructions provided in this book, will guide the teaching of breathing and breath support, phonation, registration, resonance, and articulation. Translations and phonetic transcriptions are provided for each selection to help students explore musical and emotional expression.

For a better understanding of the technical concepts employed in the selection and preparation of the repertoire that is included in this volume, please refer to:

Literature for Teaching: A Guide for Teaching Solo Vocal Repertoire from a Developmental Perspective by Christopher Arneson with Lauren Athey-Janka, Inside View Press, 2014

Acknowledgements

The authors extend their sincerest thanks to the following people:

Nicolette Biddle
Josh Bodanza
Alexander Brousseau
Andrew Gavin
Lauren Gilmore
Vicky Nooe
Mike Parisi
Kathryn Pepe
Elisabeth Pirolli
Robert Sickles
Dan Sullivan

Solo Vocal Repertoire for Singers and Teachers of Singers
Soprano Edition

Table of Contents

I.P.A. GUIDE: VOWELS

Forward vowels:	[i]	cheese	
	[ɪ]	hip	
	[e]	hey	
	[ɛ]	wed	
	[æ]	bad	
	[a]	mama	

Back vowels:	[u]	rude
	[ʊ]	hook
	[o]	rope
	[ɔ]	raw
	[ɑ]	father

Central vowels:
- [ʌ] up
- [ə] about
- [ɝ] heard, American r
- [ɒ] dare, British vocalic r
- [ɚ] never, American r

Diphthongs:
- [eɪ] wait
- [oʊ] vote
- [aɪ] wine
- [aʊ] couch
- [ɔɪ] joy
- [ju] huge

Mixed vowels:

[y]	German: *für*	French: lune
[Y]	German: *Glück*	
[ø]	German: *schön*	French: deux
[œ]	German: *könnte*	French: coeur

French Nasals:

[ɛ̃]	[ɛ] plus nasality	French: *bien* [bjɛ̃]
		English: fount**ain**
[ɑ̃]	[ɑ] plus nasality	French: *dans* [dɑ̃]
		English: ho**n**k
[õ]	[o] plus nasality	French: *bon* [bõ]
		English: **on**ly
[œ̃]	[œ] plus nasality	French: *humble* [œ̃blə]
		English: **un**cle

German Diphthongs:

[aɪ]	German: *meine*	English: mine
[ao]	German: *Augen*	English: couch
[ɔø]	German: *Freude*	English: joy

Glottal Stop:
- [ʔ] closure of glottis, as in the expression "uh-oh"

I.P.A. GUIDE: CONSONANTS

Stop plosives:	[p]	pal	*Nasals:*	[m]	mind
	[b]	back		[n]	narrow
	[t]	teach		[ŋ]	sing
	[d]	down			
	[k]	kangaroo			
	[g]	get			

Fricatives:	[f]	finger	*Lateral:*	[l]	laugh
	[v]	victory			
	[θ]	thin			
	[ð]	that			
	[s]	self			
	[z]	zebra			
	[ʃ]	ship			
	[ʒ]	azure			
	[h]	him			

Glides:	[r]	rose (American English)	*Combined:*	[tʃ]	chip
	[j]	yellow		[dʒ]	jump
	[ʍ]	what, unvoiced			
	[w]	way, voiced			

Trill, Tap, or flip:	[ɾ]	Italian: *moro* (single flip R)
	[r]	Italian: *ride* (trilled R)
	[r. r]	Italian: *terra* (prolonged trilled R)

Enya: [ɲ] English: onion Italian: *regno* [reɲɔ] French: *vignes* [viɲə]

Elya: [ʎ] English: million Italian: *figlio* [fiʎɔ]

French Glide: [ɥ] French: lui [lɥi] (pronounce [y] then quickly move to [i])

German ichlaut: [ç] English: hue German: *dich* [diç]

German achlaut: [χ] German: *nacht* [naχt]

A Basic Guide to Vocal Exercises
for Beginning Singing Teachers

The questions we are asked most frequently concern the use and function of vocal exercises, or *vocalises*. These inquiries often come from young, aspiring voice teachers and singers, so it seems appropriate to discuss their application.

One of the main reasons for using vocal exercises is to establish good singing technique. But while singing teachers likely agree that voice training must address issues of posture and alignment, respiration, phonation, registration, resonation, and articulation, there is little consensus about the specific types of exercises that should be used. Vocal exercises themselves have no intrinsic value; their effectiveness is measured by how they are applied and under what conditions they are used. Vocal exercises can be designed to help singers achieve optimal onset (initiation of the tone), placement, resonance, breath support, phrasing, legato, staccato, agility, range, vowel clarity, consonants, intonation, and coordination of registers (consecutive pitches with similar timbre that are produced with the same vocal mechanism).

Pre-phonatory exercises involving relaxation, posture, and alignment are essential. Working with students to free specific areas of tension, including muscles of the jaw, tongue, and neck, and helping them to understand the importance of a well-aligned body is the first order of business (e.g. spine elongated, neck back, sternum out, pelvis tucked under, knees unlocked).

The goal of a balanced **ONSET**, or the easy, clean initiation of tone, is usually achieved with simple exercises that feature repeated notes with a breath in between each repetition. Voiced consonants facilitate resonance, tonal efficiency, and clean, clear onsets. An audible, aspirate [h] often is used in staccato or panting exercise, quickly moving on to an inaudible, or imaginary [h].

PLACEMENT refers to the physical sensations experienced while singing. Exercises involving nasal consonants, the vowels [e] and [i], and staccato exercises using voiced consonants, often are used to increase the awareness of resonance sensations in the mask (the general area of the cheekbones).

Maximizing **RESONANCE** is one of the chief goals of classical singing; humming often is used as exercise for this purpose. The colloquial, affirmative "mm-hmm" and the nasal consonant [ng], often also are used to increase sensations of resonance, along with the sibilants [s] and [z] followed by vowels.

The coordination of expiration and phonation, called **BREATH SUPPORT** (breath management), can be developed through the use of pulsation exercises on repeated notes (e.g. [a, a, a, a]), staccato, and the *messa di voce* (crescendo-decrescendo). Lip trills also help to develop breath management skills, as do voiced sibilant and fricative consonants [z] and [v].

LEGATO is consistent phonation, uninterrupted by changing pitches or words, and is one of the most desirable aspects of beautiful singing. Glissandos (slides) can be helpful in introducing the idea of legato, followed by intervallic skip, slurring between each skip. Changing vowels on a slow scale or repeated tones with a single vowel also are useful exercises.

STACCATO is produced much in the same way as legato but without sustaining the sound between each note. Simple scales and repeated notes with a vowel preceded by [h] or [b] and simple arpeggiated chords using "hip" and "yuh" teach staccato effectively. Staccato exercises also help to develop onset and breath coordination.

PHRASING is the grouping of notes into specific units for an artistic or technical purposes. Exercises that develop legato and breath management can help to teach phrasing. Sustained scales, arpeggios and exercises with strategically placed breaths also develop the breath control skills necessary for long phrases.

AGILITY, the execution of fast moving passages with clear articulation, accuracy, and freedom, promotes flexibility and coordination and is of primary importance in good singing. Fast arpeggios and ascending/descending scales using the vowels [u] and [a] (or alternating vowels) help to develop agility.

RANGE extension is accomplished by singing ascending and descending scales and arpeggios, using five, eight, nine, eleven, and sixteen tones. A variety of vowels can be used alone and in combination.

VOWEL clarity, unification, equalization, differentiation, and evenness also must be taught. The production of a free, consistent scale throughout the vocal range with distinct, clear vowels on every pitch is paramount to good singing (voice acoustics makes this nearly impossible for women singing their highest pitches). A neutral tongue position from which all other vowels can be produced will help to develop vowel clarity. Simple arpeggios that alternate front and back vowels such as [a-o-i-o], also are useful.

CONSONANTS, especially voiced consonants, frequently are used in vocal exercises to develop coordinated onset and resonance. Scale patterns, repeated notes, arpeggios, and thirds are useful, with consonants articulated on every note. Initial, medial, and final consonants should be included, and paired unvoiced and voiced consonants are beneficial. Exercises using consonants help to create freedom and flexibility in the articulators (jaw, tongue, and lips).

Exercises for the **COORDINATION of REGISTERS** to promote a seamless, consistent vocal scale usually begin in the area just above or below the register break or *passaggio*. A vocalise consisting of two pitches moving slowly from one to the next and modulating up and down through the *passaggio* is helpful. A variety of vowels may be used on short scales, followed by short arpeggios and interval skips. Closed vowels often are used for men in the upper *passaggio* (above Middle-C, also known as C^4) and for women in the lower *passaggio* (also above Middle-C). Alternating between the vowels [u] and [a] can help singers coordinate the registers.

Descending arpeggios from the head voice in women and falsetto in men, and the use of sirens (vocal slides) also are beneficial.

Ingo Titze, one of our foremost voice scientists, lists "The Five Best Vocal Warmup Exercises" in Volume 57, No.3, 2001 of the *Journal of Singing*:

- Lip trill and tongue trill
- Two octave pitch glides
- Forward tongue roll and extension
- *Messa di voce* (crescendo-decrescendo)
- Staccato on arpeggios

By taking into account the criteria we use to judge whether a tone is functional and/or beautiful—easy onset, legato, clear diction, bright/dark tone quality, excellent breath management skills—we can make decisions as to which exercises might help students best achieve these goals. Keeping a record of what we see and hear in our initial consultation with a singer can serve as a basis for the vocalises that subsequently are developed and utilized.

Students must understand that a secure singing technique can be achieved through regular use of vocal exercises, which should be described in a simple and objective manner. All exercises should be tailored to serve the needs of individual students; few really are needed, provided every aspect of technique is addressed. Many teachers believe that it is essential to assign a specific sequence of vocal exercises, which often follow the major areas of vocal technique, including posture, respiration, phonation, resonance, support, registration, articulation. While this strategy might prove helpful, it is not required.

There are numerous books of vocalises still in print by the 19th century singing masters, including Sieber, Vaccai, Concone and Marchesi. All were well-known teachers and their exercises, along with those of contemporary authors such as William Vennard, Richard Miller, Oren Brown and James McKinney, can help young teachers get started.

A Vocal Exercise Bibliography

Brown, Oren L. (1996). *Discover Your Voice*. San Diego, CA: Singular Publishing Group, Inc.

Coffin, B. (1980). *Overtones of Bel Canto*. Metuchen, NJ: The Scarecrow Press, Inc.

Concone, J. (1898). *Thirty Daily Exercises for the Voice*. New York: G. Schirmer, Inc.

Garcia, M., II. (1975) *A Complete Treatise on the Art of Singing: Part Two* (D. V. Paschke, Ed. and Trans.). New York: Da Capo Press.

Lamperti, G. B. (1905). *The Techniques of Bel Canto* (M. Heidrich. Ed., T. Baker, Trans.). New York: G. Schirmer.

Marchesi, S. (1970) *Bel Canto: A Theoretical and Practical Vocal Method*. London: Enoch and Sons, Ltd., n.d.; reprint, New York: Dover Publications.

McKinney, J. C. (1982) *The Diagnosis and Correction of Vocal Faults*. Nashville, TN: Broadman Press.

Miller, R. (1986). *The Structure of Singing*. New York: Schirmer Books.

Reid, C. L. (1965). *The Free voice: A Guide to Natural Singing*. New York: Coleman-Ross Company, Inc.

Sieber, Ferdinand (1899). *Thirty-Six Eight-Measure Vocalises for Soprano*: op. 92: Volume 111 of Schirmer's library of music classics.

Sieber, Ferdinand (1899). *Thirty-Six Eight-Measure Vocalises for Mezzo-Soprano*: op. 93: Volume 112 of Schirmer's library of music classics.

Sieber, Ferdinand (1899). *Thirty-Six Eight-Measure Vocalises for Alto*: op. 94: Volume 113 of Schirmer's library of music classics.

Sieber, Ferdinand (1899). *Thirty-Six Eight-Measure Vocalises for Tenor*: op. 95: Volume 114 of Schirmer's library of music classics.

Sieber, Ferdinand (1899). *Thirty-Six Eight-Measure Vocalises for Baritone*: op. 96: Volume 115 of Schirmer's library of music classics.

Sieber, Ferdinand (1899). *Thirty-Six Eight-Measure Vocalises for Bass*: op. 97: Volume 116 of Schirmer's library of music classics.

Vennard, W. (1967). *Singing: The Mechanism and the Technic* (rev. ed.). Boston: Carl Fischer, Inc.

Tanto Sospirerò

Italian
Pietro Paolo Bencini

Respiration and Support

In the beginning of vocal studies, it may be necessary to add in more breaths while respiration and support skills are being mastered. In measures 9-12, insert a breath after *faro*, and then remove it later when breathing improves.

Resonance

In measure 13, utilize the high sensations of resonance from the consonant [m] to create flexibility as the soprano approaches the *passaggio* (transition area). The lips are gently touching and there should be space between the teeth when creating [m].

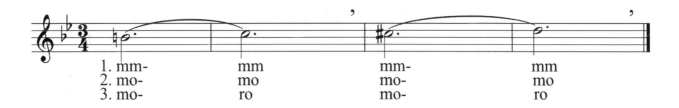

Phonation

Insert [a] before the word *tanto*, which will help to maintain the correct vowel space for the phrase. The consonant should be created in the vowel space.

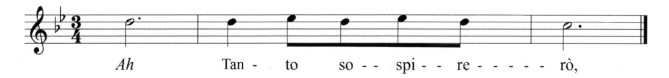

Registration

This melody ascends and descends to and from the *passaggio*, building vocal strength and coordination. Begin to work through the *passaggio* with rounded vowels, and then transition to vowel-to-vowel singing.

1. [u]
2. [o]
3. [a - o - o - i - e - ɔ]   [a - o - i - a - e - ɔ]
4. [a - o - i - a - e - ɔ]   [a - o - o - i - e - ɔ]

Diction/Articulation-

Practice the text with a free jaw and an independent tongue, first spoken, and then sung on a single pitch, and finally with the melody. Careful attention should be given to the dental consonants, which are created only with the tongue: [t], [r] and [l].

Slowly speak: *Tanto sospirerò, tanto mi lagnerò*, and then sing:

Phonetic Transcription and Translation of the Text

Tanto   sospirerò,
[ˈtan.to   so.spi.ɾe.ˈɾɔ]
I will sigh greatly,

Tanto   mi   lagnerò,
[tan.to   mi   laɲ.ɲe.ˈɾɔ]
I will languish greatly,

Che   intender   le   faro,
[ke   in.ˈtɛn.der   le   ˈfaː.ɾo]
So to make her understand

Che   per   lei   moro!
[ke   per   lɛːi   ˈmɔː.ɾo]
That I would die for her!

Pur   l'alma   le   dirà:
[puːr   ˈlal.ma   le   di.ˈɾa]
Even my soul will say:

"Cara,   t'adoro!"
[ˈkaːra   ta.ˈdoː.ɾo]
"My dear, I adore you!"

Tanto   sospirerò,
[ˈtan.to   so.spi.ɾe.ˈɾɔ]
I will sigh greatly

Tanto   mi   lagnerò,
[ˈtan.to   mi   laɲ.ɲe.ˈɾɔ]
I will languish greatly

Che   intender   le   faro,
[ke   in.ˈtɛn.der   le   ˈfaː.ɾo]
So to make her understand

Che   per   lei   moro!
[ke   per   lɛːi   ˈmɔː.ɾo]
That I would die for her!

Tanto Sospirerò

Pietro Paolo Benicini
(1700-1755)

Tan - to so-spi-re - rò,

Tan-to mi la-gne - rò, Che in - ten - der le fa - rò, Che per lei mo - ro,

mo - ro, mo - ro, Che in - ten - der le fa - rò, Che per lei

mo - ro, Che in - ten - der le fa - rò, Che per lei mo - ro!

Pur l'al - ma le di - rà:___ "Ca - ra, t'a-do - ro! Ca-ra, ca - ra, t'a-do-

ro!" Tan-to so-spi-re - rò, Tan-to mi la-gne - rò, Che in - ten - der le fa

rò, Che per lei mo - ro, mo - ro, mo -

ro, Che in - ten - der le fa - rò, Che per lei mo - rò, Che in - ten - der le fa

rò, Che per lei mo - ro!

col canto

a tempo, morendo

Se bel rio

Italian
Raffaello Rontani

Respiration and Support

The sibiliant [s] and fricative [f] appear frequently in the text. Using the rhythm of the melody, insert spoken [s] and [f] to facilitate the movement of the breath, which helps to articulate the rhythm with the muscles of breath support.

Resonance

Extract the vowels from the text while singing the opening melody. Repeat this exercise throughout the song. Keep the feeling of vowel-to-vowel legato as you sing the actual text. Final consonants should be as late as possible and should not interrupt the purity of the vowels.

Phonation

Words ending in vowels provide an excellent opportunity to teach coordinated offsets. In mid-range, practice this exercise to develop efficient offsets. If the offset includes a sudden burst of escaping air, closing the mouth or inserting a decrescendo might prove helpful.

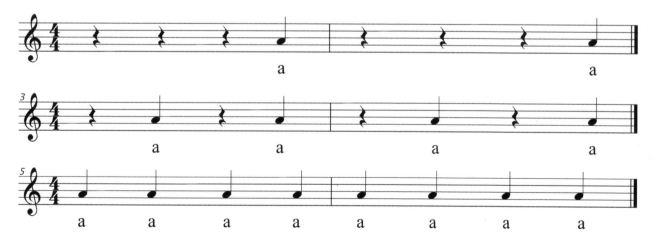

Registration

In the second verse, interpolated melismas assist in maintaining balance of registration. As you practice, employ a variety of vowels and sing the melismas from the melody in the second verse.

Diction/Articulation

Follow this four-step exercise to develop flexibility of articulation:

1. In a simple rhythm, speak the text of the second verse.
2. In a simple rhythm, sing the text on one pitch.
3. Speak the text in the rhythm of the melody.
4. Sing the text with the written melody.

Phonetic Transcription and Translation of the Text

Se bel rio, se bell'auretta fra l'erbetta
[se bɛl riːo se bɛl.laːu.ˈrɛt.ta fra lɛr.ˈbɛt.ta]
If a beautiful brook, or a beautiful breeze

Sul mattin mormorand'erra;
[sul mat.ˈtiːn mɔr.mo.ran.ˈdɛr.ra]
wanders in the morning among the tender grasses;

Se di fiori un praticello si fa bello,
[se di ˈfjoː.ri un pra.ti.ˈtʃɛl.lo si fa ˈbɛl.lo]
if a little meadow adorns itself with flowers,

Noi diciam ride la terra.
[noːi di.ˈtʃaːm ˈriː.de la ˈtɛr.ra]
we say the earth is smiling.

Quando avvien che un zeffiretto per diletto
[ˈkwan.do av.ˈvjɛːn ke un zef.fi.ˈrɛt.o per di.lɛt.to]
When for pleasure, a little breeze

Bagni il piè nell'onde chiare,
[ˈba. ‿ ɲil pjɛ nɛl.ˈlon.de ˈkjaː.re]
bathes its feet in the clear waters,

Sì che l'acqua su l'arena scherzo appena,
[si ke ˈla.kwa su la.ˈreː.na ˈsker.tso ap.ˈpeː.na]
so that the water scarcely touches the sand,

Noi diciam che ride il mare.
[noːi di.ˈtʃaːm ke ˈriː.de il ˈmaː.re]
we say the sea is smiling.

Se bel rio

from *Le varie musiche*

Raffaello Rontani
(15??-1622)

Se bel rio, se bel - l'au - ret - ta fra l'er -

bet - ta__ sul mat - tin mor - mo - ran - d'er - ra; se di

fio - ri un pra - ti - cel-lo si fa bel - lo, noi di - ciam: ri - de___ la ter - ra.

Quando av - vien che un Zef - fi - ret - to___ per di - let - to___ bagni il

piè___nell' on - de_ chia - re, sì che l'ac - qua su l'a-

re - na scher-zi a pe — na, noi di- ciam che ri — de il ma - re.

Lieblingsplätzchen

German
Felix Mendelssohn

Respiration and Support

Breath patterns often are predictable in pieces with three/four meter. Consonants in German also provide opportunity for coordinated breath support. For example, in the first sentence, *Wisst ihr wo ich gerne weil'*, elongate the [v] in *wisst, wo, weil,* and the [g] in *gerne,* and encourage engagement of the rib and abdominal muscles. Sing this phrase, as written below:

Resonance

It is necessary to maintain consistent resonance when vowels change quickly and when the same vowel is sung on a variety of pitches. Practice first singing a single vowel, and then vowel-to-vowel, as shown below.

Phonation

The vowels [i] and [ɪ] frequently appear in the text of this piece. Practice these vowels using spoken and sung staccati. A high sensation of resonance is felt for both vowels. Engage the abdominal muscles when practicing the exercise below to close the glottis for the onset.

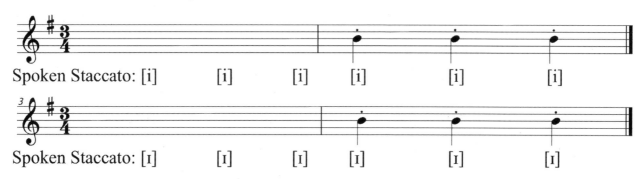

Registration

It is necessary to maintain a smooth transition between the middle and upper voice. Using the music from measures 11-12, practice short ascending scales, moving up by half-steps . Utilize a slur to ease coordination.

[i]
[e]
[a]
[o]
[u]

Diction/Articulation

Syllabic settings present challenges in the area of articulation. Gently place a finger on the chin to isolate and bring attention to the muscles of the jaw, which should remain free and relatively relaxed. The tongue is active in pronouncing consonants and vowels. Speak and sing through the text at varying speeds while watching the mouth in a mirror. This exercise increases awareness of the muscles of articulation: lips, tongue and jaw.

Notice that many German words end with a *schwa* sound: [ə]. This is a unique speech sound in German that requires practice. Many American singers incorrectly use the wrong sounds. This was Lindsey Christiansen's[1] explanation of *Schwa*:

> After bright vowels, shaded toward [ɛ]: liebe, schwebe
> After rounded vowels, shaded toward rounded [ə]: möchte, rufe
> When these sounds appear at the end of a word: en, el, es, et, er, shaded toward darker [ə]: Himmel, Mutter

---

[1] Professor Christiansen was a prominent singing teacher who spent most of her career teaching at Westminster Choir College

Phonetic Transcription and Translation of the Text

Wißt ihr, wo ich gerne weil'
[vɪst ʔiːɐ̯ voː ʔɪç ˈgɛr.ne vaːel]
Do you know where I gladly stay

In der Abendkühle?
[ʔɪn deːɐ̯ ˈʔaːbənt.ˌkyː.lə]
in the evening coolness?

In dem stillen Tale geht
[ʔɪn deːm ˈʃtɪ.lən ˈtaː.lə geːt]
In the peaceful valley turns

Eine kleine Mühle,
[ˈʔaːe.nə ˈklaːe.nə ˈmyː.lə]
a small mill,

Und ein kleiner Bach da bei,
[ʔʊnt ʔaːen ˈklaːe.nɐ baχ daˌ ˈbaːe]
and a small brook passes,

Rings umher steh'n Bäume.
[rɪŋs ʔʊm.ˈheːɐ̯ ʃteːn ˈbɔːʏ.mə]
around the grove of trees.

Oft sitz' ich da stundenlang,
[ʔɔft zɪts ʔɪç daː ˈʃtʊn.dən.laŋ]
I often sit there for hours,

Schau' umher und träume.
[ʃaːo ʔʊm.ˈheːɐ̯ ʔʊnt ˈtrɔːʏ.mə]
gazing about and dreaming.

Auch die Blümlein in dem Grün
[ʔaːoχ diː ˈblyːm.laːen ʔɪn deːm gryːn]
Also the little flowers in the grass

An zu sprechen fangen,
[ʔan tsuː ˈʃprɛ.çən ˈfa.ŋən]
begin to speak.

Und das blaue Blümlein sagt;
[ʔʊnt das ˈblaːu.ə ˈblyːm.laːen zaːkt]
And the blue little flower says;

Sieh' mein Köpfchen hangen!
[ziː maːen ˈkœpf.çən ˈha.ŋən]
Look at my little hanging head!

Röslein mit dem Dornenkuss
[røːz.laːen mɪt deːm ˈdɔr.nən.ˌkus]
The little rose with the thorny kiss

Hat mich so gestochen:
[hat mɪç zoː gə.ˈʃtɔ.χən]
has pricked me so:

Ach! das macht mich gar betrübt,
[ʔax das maχt mɪç gaːɐ bə.ˈtryːpt]
Ah! That makes me very sad,

Hat mein Herz gebrochen.
[hat maːen hɛrts gə.ˈbrɔ.χən]
It has broken my heart.

Da naht sich ein Spinnlein weiß,
[daː naːt zɪç ʔaːen ˈʃpɪn.laːən vaːes]
A little white spider draws near,

Spricht Sei doch zufrieden;
[ʃprɪçt zaːe dɔχ tsu.ˈfriː.dən]
it says: Be contented;

Einmal musst du doch vergeh'n
[ˈʔaːen.maːl mʊst du dɔχ fɛɐ̯.ˈgeːn]
some day you must surely die,

So ist es hienieden;
[zoː ʔɪst ʔɛs hi.ˈniː.dən]
So it is here on earth;

Besser, dass das herz dir bricht
[ˈbɛ.sɐ das das hɛrts diːɐ̯ brɪçt]
it is better to suffer a broken heart

Von dem Kuss der Rose,
[fɔn deːm kʊs deːɐ̯ ˈroː.zə]
from the kiss of a rose,

Als du kennst die Liebe nicht
[ʔals duː kɛnst diː ˈliː.bə nɪçt]
than to have never known love

Und stirbst liebelose
[ʔʊnt ʃtɪrpst ˈliː.bə.loː.zə]
and die without it.

Lieblingsplätzchen

Op. 99, No. 3

Friederike Robert

Felix Mendelssohn
(1809-1847)

Oft sitz ich da stun-den-lang, schau um-her und träu - - - - - - me.
ach! das macht mich gar be-trübt, hat mein Herz ge - bro - - - - - chen.
als du kennst die Lie-be nicht und stirbst lie-be - lo - - - - - se.

Jasminenstrauch

German
Robert Schumann

Respiration and Support

Six/eight meter often offers regular opportunities to replenish breath silently. We have added an eighth-rest in the marked measures to allow singers to take a silent catch breath through [a] shape, and to set the position for the following measure. A catch breath is felt quickly both up and down: the soft palate lifts and the abdominal muscles release.

Grün ist der Jas - min - nen - strauch A - bends ein - ge - schla - fen

Resonance

The technical goal is to learn to sustain consistent resonance while frequently changing vowels. Pronounce the text slowly, elongating the vowels while maintaining sensations of resonance.

i.e. [gryyyyːn ʔɪɪɪɪst deeeeːɒ jaaasː'miiiiiːːnəəən ʃtraaaaːoooχ]

Phonation

In the German language, it is necessary to employ a gentle glottal onset when a word begins with a vowel. Practice a harsh glottal onset, followed by a soft glottal onset, and then one in between, so that the glottis is firmly closed before the vowels. This closure can be felt when saying "ouch." If there is a struggle to find this closure, singing the vocal line below will close the glottis.

[ng]

Registration

This song assists in balancing middle voice registration. Frequent dotted rhythms, combined with slurs, help the vocal folds to find flexibility and appropriate adjustments. Practice this skill by singing vowel-to-vowel.

[y - ɪ - eːɒ - a - i - ə - aːo - a - ə - a - e - ə - a - ə]

Diction/Articulation

Practice consonant clusters by gently mouthing the words, lightly whispering the words, adding a resonant voice, and finally adding pitch. Teach diction apart from voice and singing.

[gry:n]
[jas:ˈmi::nən]
[ʃtra:oχ]
[a::bənts]
[a:en:gə:ʃla::fən]

[als]
[mɔr:gəns]
[zɔn:nən]
[lɪç:tɒ]
[tra::fən]

Phonetic Transcription and Translation of the Text

Grün   ist   der   Jasminenstrauch
[gry:n   ʔist   de:ɐ̯   jas.ˈmi:.nən. ʃtra:uχ]
Green is the jasmine bush

Abends   eingeschlafen,
[ˈʔa:.bənts   ˈʔa:en.gə.ʃla:.fən]
in the evening when it fell asleep,

Als   ihn   mit   des   Morgens   Hauch
[ʔals   ʔi:n   mɪt   dɛs   ˈmɔr.gəns   ha:uχ]
And when, with the breath of morning,

Sonnenlichter   trafen
[ˈzɔ.nən.ˌlɪç.tɒ   ˈtra:.fən]
It was struck with the sun's rays,

Ist   er   schneeweiß   aufgewacht:
[ʔɪst   ʔe:ɐ̯   ˈʃne:.ˌva:es   ˈʔa:of.gə.vaχt]
it awakened as white as snow:

"Wie   geschah   mir   in   der   Nacht?"
[vi: gə.ˈʃa: mi:ɐ̯   ʔin   de:ɐ̯   naχt]
"What happened to me in the night?"

Seht   so   geht   es   Bäumen,
[ze:t   zo: ge:t   ʔɛs   ˈbɔ:ɤ.mən]
See, so it is with trees,

Die   im   Frühling   träumen.
[di: ʔɪm   ˈfry:lɪŋ   ˈtrɔ:ɤ.mən]
which dream in the spring.

Jasminenstrauch

Op. 27, No. 4

F. Rückert

Robert Schumann
(1810-1856)

Grün___ ist der Jas - mi - nen-strauch A - bends ein - ge-schla - fen. Als ihn mit des Mor - gens Hauch Son - nen- lich - ter tra - fen, ist er schnee-weiß auf - ge-wacht:

"Wie ge-schah mir in der Nacht?" Seht, so geht es

Bäu - men,— die im Früh - ling träu - men.

Le mariage des roses

French
César Franck

Respiration and Support

Sing a variety of sustained vowels to propel the breath above the reiterated sixteenth-note pattern in the right-hand of the piano accompaniment. This movement should inspire engagement in the abdominal muscles.

Sing these four pitches with the marked crescendi and decrescendi on the following vowels:

[i], [e], [a] [o] and [u]

Resonance

Maintaining an elevated soft palate while singing in French can be difficult at the beginning of vocal studies. To balance resonance, sing a pure vowel on one pitch, followed by the parallel nasal vowel, and then return to the pure vowel. The palate should be lifted for the non-nasal vowel, but will drop for the nasalized versions.

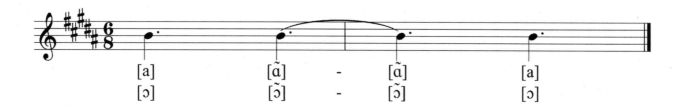

Phonation

Words sung in French often end in a vowel sound, followed by a consonant in the next word. Practice this song maintaining a sense of openness in the throat, just as you feel in the beginning of a yawn, as you move from vowel to consonant.

Registration

For acoustic reasons, sopranos often need to open the vowels slightly when ascending to the top of the staff and beyond. This text provides opportunities to practice that skill because of the closed and nasal vowels found in the French language.

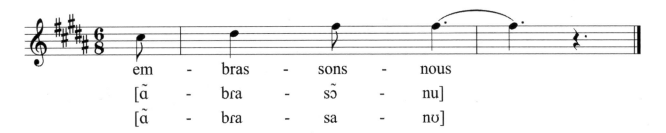

Diction/Articulation

The French sound [y] demands that the tongue be in the [i] position and the lips be in the [u] position. In this exercise, practice flexibility in articulation. Move slowly from [i] to [u] and [u] to [i], allowing the jaw to be free. This prepares the quick action needed to create the French sound [y].

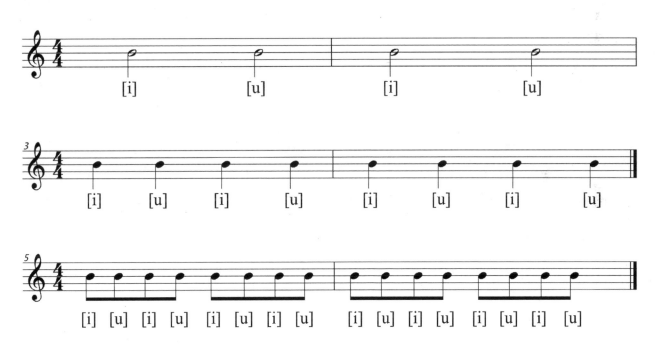

Phonetic Transcription and Translation of the Text

Mignonne, sais tu comment,
[mi.ɲɔ.nə   sɛ   ty   kɔ.mã]
Darling, do you know,

S'épousent les roses?
[se.pu.zə   le   ɾo.zə]
how the roses marry?

Ah! cet hymen est charmant!
[a   sɛ.‿ti.mɛ.‿nɛ   ʃaɾ.mã]
Ah! The marriage is charming!

Quelles tendres choses
[kɛ.lə   tã.dɾə   ʃo.zə]
What tender things

Elles disent en ouvrant
[ɛ.lə   di.zə.‿tã.‿nu.vɾã]
they say when they open

Leurs paupières closes!
[løɾ   po.pjɛ.ɾə   klo.zə]
their closed eyes!

Mignonne, sais tu comment,
[mi.ɲɔ.nə   sɛ   ty   kɔ.mã]
Darling, do you know,

S'épousent les roses?
[se.pu.zə   le   ɾozə]
how the roses marry?

Elles disent: Aimons nous!
[ɛ.lə   di.zə   ɛ.mõ   nu]
They say: Let us love one another!

Si courte est la vie!
[si   kuɾ.‿tɛ   la   vi.ə]
Life is so short!

Ayons les baisers plus doux,
[ɛ.jõ   le   be.ze   ply   du]
Let us have the sweetest kisses

L'âme plus ravie!
[la.mə   ply   ɾa.vi.ə]
the most delighted soul!

Pendant que l'homme, à genoux,
[pã.dã   kə   lɔ.‿ma   ʒə.nu]
While the man, on bended knee

Doute, espère, ou prie!
[dut.‿ɛs.pɛ.‿ɾu   pri.ə]
doubts, hopes, or prays!

Ô mes soeurs, embrassons-nous
[o   mɛ   sœɾ.‿ã.bɾa.sõ.nu]
Oh my sisters, let us embrace

Si courte est la vie!
[si   kuɾ.‿tɛ   la   vi.ə]
Life is so short!

Croix-moi, mignonne, croix-moi,
[kɾwa.mwa   mi.ɲõ.nə   kɾwa.mwa]
Believe me, my darling, believe me,

Aimons nous comme elles,
[ɛ.mõ   nu   kɔ.‿mɛ.lə]
let us love one another as they do,

Vois, le printemps vient à toi,
[vwa   lə   pɾẽ.tã   vjẽ.‿ta   twa]
look, the spring comes to you,

Et, des hirondelles
[e   de.‿zi.ɾõ.dɛ.lə]
and for the swallows

Aimer est l'unique loi
[ɛ.me.ɾɛ ly.ni.kə lwa]
love is the only law

À leurs nids fidèles.
[a lœr ni fi.dɛ.lə]
in their faithful nests.

Ô ma reine suis ton roi,
[o ma ɾɛ.nə sɥi tõ ɾwa]
Oh my queen, I am your king,

Aimons nous comme elles.
[ɛ.mõ nu kɔ.͜mɛ.lə]
let us love one another as they do.

Excepté d'avoir aimé,
[ɛk.sɛp.te da.vwa.ɾɛ.me]
Except for love

Qu'est-il donc sur terre?
[kɛ.til dõ syɾ tɛ.ɾə]
what else is there in the world?

Notre horizon est fermé,
[nɔ.͜tɾɔ.ri.zõ.͜nɛ fɛr.me]
Our horizon is closed,

Ombre, nuit, mystère!
[õ.bɾə nɥi mis.tɛ.ɾə]
shadow, night, mystery !

Un seul phare est allumé,
[œ̃ søl fa.͜ɾɛ.͜ta.ly.me]
One beacon is lit,

L'amour nous l'éclaire!
[la.muɾ nu le.klɛ.ɾə]
love is our guiding light!

Excepté d'avoir aimé,
[ɛk.sɛp.te da.vwa.ɾɛ.me]
Except for love

Qu'est-il donc sur terre?
[kɛ.til dõ syɾ tɛ.ɾə]
what else is there in the world?

25

Le Mariage des Roses

Eugène David

César Franck
(1822-1890)

ro - - ses? El - les di - sent: ai - mons- nous!__ __ Si courte est la vi - e! Ay - ons les bai - sers plus doux,_____ L'â - me plus ra - vi - e! Pen - dant que l'homme à ge - noux_____ Doute, es - père ou

moi, Ai-mons - nous comme el - les, Vois, le prin-temps vient à

toi,_____ Le prin-temps vient à toi,_____

Et des hi - ron - del - les; Ai - mer est l'u - ni - que

loi_____ A leurs nids_____ fi - dè - les. Ô ma

cresc

al - lu - mé,_____ L'a - mour nous l'é - clai - re.

Ex - cep - té d'a - voir ai - mé,_____ Qu'est-il donc sur ter - re?

La Brise

French
Camille Saints-Saëns

Respiration and Support

Short note values and tempo markings such as *Allegro lusingando* (brisk and caressing) facilitate flexibility in the muscles of breathing. Rhythmic pronunciation of the text, spoken gently and forward in the mouth, creates flexibility in the intercostal and abdominal muscles. This type of song is excellent for students whose breath may lock in sustained phrases.

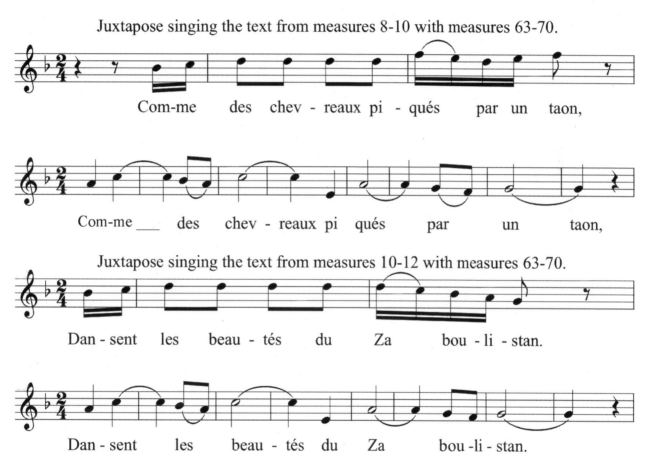

Juxtapose singing the text from measures 8-10 with measures 63-70.

Com-me   des   chev - reaux pi - qués   par un taon,

Com-me___ des   chev - reaux pi qués   par   un   taon,

Juxtapose singing the text from measures 10-12 with measures 63-70.

Dan - sent   les   beau - tés   du   Za   bou - li - stan.

Dan - sent   les   beau - tés   du   Za   bou -li - stan.

Resonance

Practice the short melismas in measures 20 and 30 on one vowel. Address the resonance through the unique speech sounds of the French language, including nasals and mixed vowels.

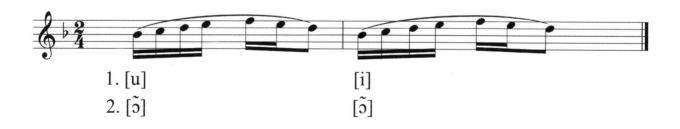

1. [u]   [i]
2. [ɔ̃]   [ɔ̃]

Phonation

The melodic writing is sequenced with dotted rhythms followed by fluid rhythms. Utilize various vowels to support this skill.

1. [u]
2. [o]
3. [ɔ]

Registration

The melismas in measures 59 and 60 encourage flexibility and coordination in the lower *passaggio*. Practice these measures singing on closed vowels in various keys around and in the lower *passaggio*.

Sing this exercise starting on G, as notated, and then F#, then F and finally on E.

1. [i]
2. [e]
3. [u]

Diction/Articulation

Students should develop an accurate perception of the sounds of the French language. Mimicry from examples of French politicians and actors found on YouTube or in movies can be helpful for developing the ear for these new sounds. Have the student mimic what she hears… and, have fun!

Phonetic Transcription and Translation of the Text

Comme des chevreaux piqués par un taon
[kɔ.mə de ʃəv.ɾo pi.ke pa.‿ɾœ̃ tɑ̃]
As children stung by a horsefly,

Dansent les beautés du Zaboulistan.
[dɑ̃.sə le bo.te dy za.bu.li.stɑ̃]
the beauties of Zaboulistan dance.

D'un rose léger sont teintés leurs ongles;
[dœ̃ ɾo.zə le.ʒe sõ tɛ̃.te lœɾ.‿zõg.lə]
With light pink polish on their nails;

Nul ne peut les voir, hormis leur sultan.
[nyl nə pø le vwaɾ ˈɔɾ.mi løɾ syl.tɑ̃]
none may see them, except their sultan.

Aux mains de chacune un sistre résonne;
[o mɛ̃ də ʃa.ky.‿nœ̃ sis.tɾə ɾe.zɔ.nə]
In the hands of each is a ringing sistrum;

Sabre au poing se tient l'eunuque en turban.
[sɑ.‿bɾo pwɛ̃ sə tjɛ̃ lø.ny.‿ kɑ̃ tyɾ.bɑ̃]
Sword in hand, the eunuch wearing a turban stands guard.

Mais du fleuve pâle où le lys sommeille
[mɛ dy flø.və pɑ.lə u lə lis sɔ.mɛ.jə]
But from the pale river where the lilies slumber,

Sort le vent nocturne ainsi qu'un forban.
[sɔɾ lə vɑ̃ nɔk.tyɾ.‿ nɛ̃.si kœ̃ fɔɾ.bɑ̃]
the night wind stirs like a pirate.

Il s'en va charmer leurs cœurs et leurs lèvres,
[il sɑ̃ va ʃaɾ.me lœɾ kœɾ.‿ze lœɾ lɛv.ɾə]
He is off to charm their hearts and their lips,

Sous l'œil du jaloux, malgré le firman.
[su lœj dy ʒa.lu mal.gɾe lə fiɾ.mɑ̃]
under the jealous man's eye, despite the law.

Ô rêveur, sois fier! Elle a, cette brise,
[o ɾɛ.vøɾ swa fje ɛ.‿la sɛ.tə bɾi.zə]
Oh dreamer, be proud! The breeze

Pris tes vers d'amour pour son talisman!
[pɾi te vɛɾ da.muɾ puɾ sõ ta.lis.mɑ̃]
has taken your love song for her talisman.

La Brise

Mélodies Persanes, Op. 26

Armand Renaud

Camille Saint-Saëns
(1835-1921)

Allegro lusingando ♩ = 92

Com-me des chev-reaux pi - qués_ par un taon, Dan-sent

les beau-tés du Za_bou-li-stan.

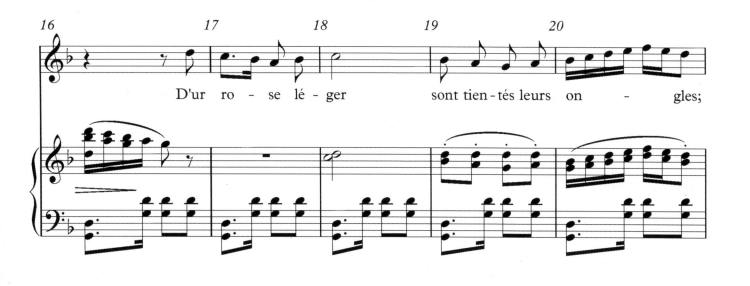

D'ur ro - se lé - ger sont tien-tés leurs on - gles;

Nul ne peut les voir, hor-mis leur sul - tan.

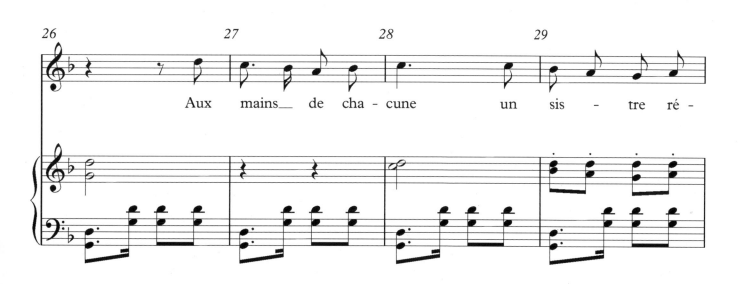

Aux mains__ de cha - cune un sis - tre ré -

son - ne; Sabre au poing, se tient l'eu - nuque en tur- ban.

Mais du fleu - ve pâ-le où le lys som- meil -

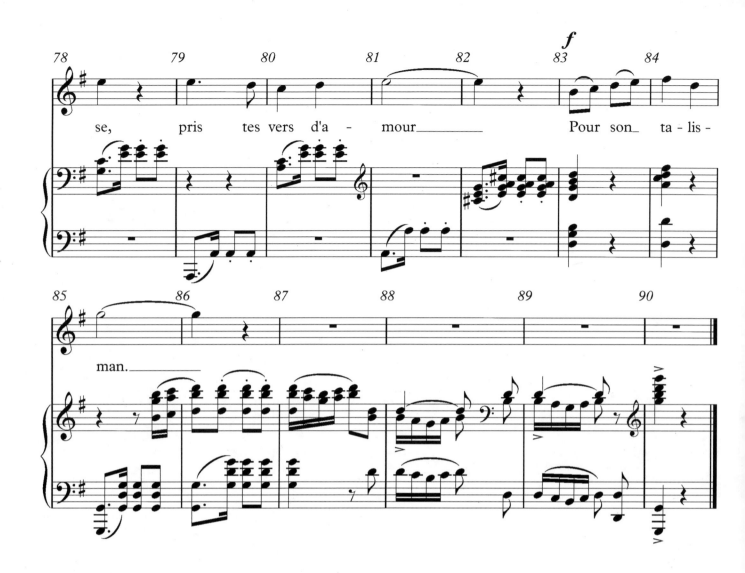

se, pris tes vers d'a - mour_____ Pour son_ ta - lis-

man._____

If You Only Knew

English
Ernest Charles

Respiration and Support
Inhale through the vowel shape of the first word of the phrase, low and deep. For example:
>   Breathe in [a] before "I think of you"
>   Breath in [ae] before "And ev'ry feathered"
>   Breathe in [u] before "With every"

Resonance
The syllabic text setting and the tessitura will strengthen and solidify resonance in the lower middle range.

Speak the text in rhythm in the pitch area of the melody, following the contour of the melody. Find a clear, resonant quality that is close to speech, but still intoned in pitch. This should feel similar to a speech-derived chant.

Phonation
The syllabic setting of the text may invite a tendency to use straight tone singing (without any vibrato). To ensure constant vibrancy and lyricism, sing this melody with the following semi-occluded exercises: [v], [m], lip or tongue trill, and through a straw.

Next, sing a phrase on one of the semi-occluded exercises, for example [v], and then sing that phrase with the text.

Do this throughout the phrases of the song, working for continued vibrancy.

Registration
To deal with the composer's request of *messa di voce* (crescendo-decrescendo), use vocalises in middle voice that include the vowels from the text.

And ev'ry feather'd chorister awakes
[æ ɛ i ɛ ɒ o ɪ ɒ a e]

Articulation/Diction
It is important to discuss elocution for text found in repertoire from this period, which requires excellent diction and articulation.

Elocution: Ask the student to read the poem with strict attention to clear and expressive speech.

This poem presents vocabulary that is not in the current vernacular; therefore, specific words might need definitions and attention from the student.

Phonetic Transcription of the Text

I	think	of	you	at	dawn,	when	morning	breaks
[aːI	θɪnk	ʌv	ju	æt	dɔn	ʍɛn	'mɔɐ̯.nɪŋ	bɹeːɪks]

And	ev'ry	feather'd	chorister	awakes;
[ænd	'ɛv.ɾi	'fɛ.ð3d	'kɔɐ̯.stɐ	ə.'weːɪks]

With	ev'ry	blade	of	grass	aglint	with	dew,
[wɪθ	'ɛv.ɾi	bleːɪd	ʌv	gɹæs	ə.'glɪnt	wɪθ	du]

I	think	of	you.
[aːI	θɪnk	ʌv	ju]

I	think	of	you	at	noon	when	clouds	float	by,
[aɪ	θɪnk	ʌv	ju	æt	nun	ʍɛn	klaːʊdz	floːʊt	baːɪ]

Across	the	azure	background	of	the	sky;
[ə.'kɾɔs	ðʌ	'æ.ʒɐ̯	'bæk.gɹaːʊnd	ʌv	ðe	skaːɪ]

And,	as	I	look	into	that	wealth	of	blue,
[ænd	æz	aːɪ	lʊk	ɪn.'tu	ðæt	wɛlθ	ʌv	blu]

I	think	of	you.
[aːI	θɪnk	ʌv	ju]

But	when	the	darkness	puts	the	day	to	flight,
[bʌt	ʍɛn	ðʌ	'daɐ̯k.nəs	pʊts	ðʌ	deːɪ	tu	flaːɪt]

I	gaze	upon	the	glories	of	the	night;
[aːɪ	geːɪz	ə.'pɑn	ðʌ	'glɔ.ɾiz	ʌv	ðʌ	naːɪt]

Then	more	than	ever,	if	you	only	knew,
[ðɛn	mɔɐ̯	ðæn	'ɛ.vɐ̯	ɪf	ju	'oːʊn.li	nu]

I	think	of	you,	of	you	alone.
[aːI	θɪnk	ʌv	ju	ʌv	ju	ə.'loːʊn]

Page intentionally left blank to facilitate page turns

If You Only Knew

George Johnston-Jervis

Ernest Charles
(1895-1984)

you.

poco rit.

mf

But when the dark-ness puts the day to flight,— I gaze up-on the

a tempo

mf

glo-ries of the night; Then more than e-ver, if you on - ly knew,

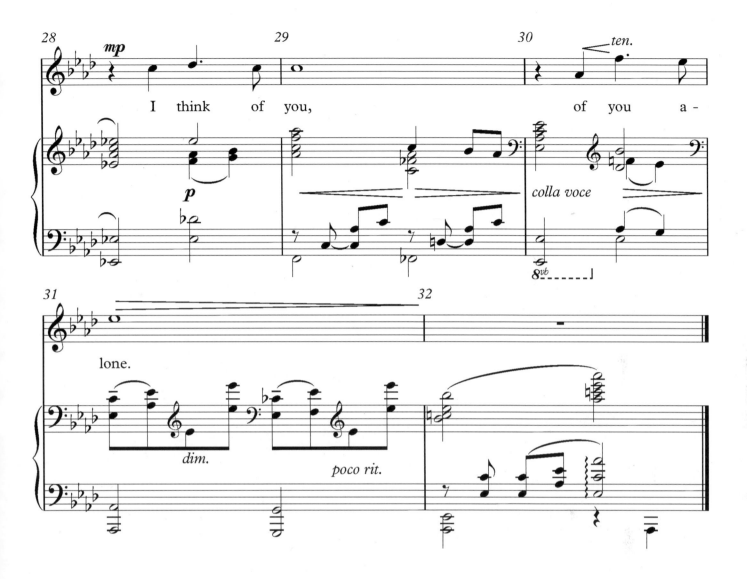

I think of you, of you a-

lone.

Symphony in Yellow

English
Charles T. Griffes

To encourage the singer to develop a musical ear, direct her to notate the *solfège* syllables in the chromatic passages of the melody. She also should memorize the *solfège* to gain confidence of pitch and pitch relationships.

Respiration and Support
Sing the opening vocal line with eighth-note subdivision on staccato [i] vowels to feel a pulse in the breath. The staccati will help to coordinate engagement in the abdominal muscles and glottal closure.

Resonance
Notice the repeated notes in this song. Choosing an important one, such as C-sharp[5], begin singing on [ng], and then practice the vowels slowly to obtain consistent resonance.

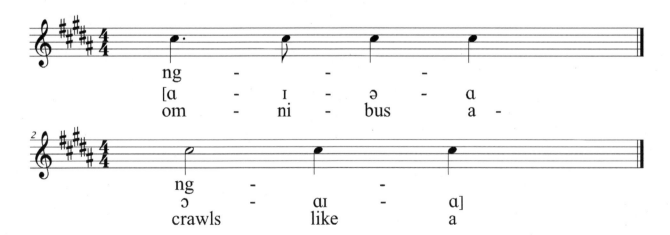

Phonation

Use "blenders" to help with onsets, taking time to differentiate where there is a stop and where sounds are connected together.

"An‿omnibus" (add slur between the words)

"Like‿a" (add slur between the words)

"Hangs‿along" (add slur between the words)

"A ‖ rod" (add tracks between the words)

"And ‖ at" (add tracks between the words)

Registration

This piece challenges the lower *passaggio*. In the example "along the quay," closed vowels help to coordinate the head and chest registers. Practice the closed vowels in this line, feeling the coordination of the lower register on the closed vowel of "quay," and then move to the last line and find that same coordination within the open vowels "a rod of ripples."

Practice the closed vowels in the 1st line, then find that same coordination in the 2nd line.

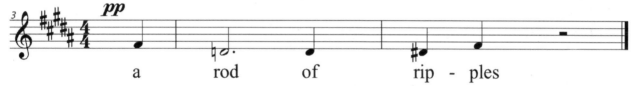

Diction/Articulation

- Take note of the double consonants in "yellow," "butterfly," "passerby," "restless," and "rippled." Use these double consonants as a diction exercise.
- Word ownership exercises: Onomatopoeia! The singer must have a mental picture of the words, so that each word sounds like its meaning.

Phonetic Transcription of the Text

An omnibus across the bridge
[æn 'ɑm.nɪ.b̥ʌs ə.'kɹɔs ðʌ bɹɪd͡ʒ]

Crawls like a yellow butterfly,
[kɹɔlz laːɪk ʌ jɛ.loːʊ 'bʌ.tɜ.flaːɪ]

And, here and there, a passer-by
[ænd hɪɐ̯ ænd ðɛɐ̯ ʌ pæ.sɜ.'baːɪ]

Shows like a little restless midge.
[ʃoːʊz laːɪk ʌ 'lɪ.təl 'ɹɛst.ləs mɪd͡ʒ]

Big barges full of yellow hay,
[bɪg 'bɑɐ̯.d͡ʒəz fʌl ʌv 'jɛ.loːʊ heːɪ]

Are moved against the shadowy wharf,
[ɑɐ̯ muvd ə.'gɛnst ðʌ 'ʃæ.doːʊ.i ʍɔɐ̯f]

And, like a yellow silken scarf,
[ænd laːɪk ʌ 'jɛ.loːʊ 'sɪl.kən skaɐ̯f

The thick fog hangs along the quay.
[ðʌ θɪk fɔg hæŋz ə.'lɔŋ ðʌ keːɪ]

The yellow leaves begin to fade,
[ðʌ 'jɛ.loːʊ livz bə.'gɪn toːʊ feːɪd]

And flutter from the temple elms,
[ænd 'flʌ.tɐ̯ fɹɑm ðʌ 'tɛm.pəl ɛlmz]

And at my feet the pale green Thames
[ænd æt maːɪ fit ðʌ peːɪl gɹin tɛmz]

Lies like a rod of rippled jade.
[laːɪz laːɪk ʌ ɹɑd ʌv 'ɹɪ.pəld jeːɪd]

Page intentionally left blank to facilitate page turns

Symphony in Yellow

Op. 3, No. 2

Oscar Wilde

Charles T. Griffes
(1884-1920)

An om - ni-bus a - cross the bridge Crawls like a yel - low but-ter-fly, And, here and there, a pass-er- by____

Quando si trovano

Aria from *Il mondo della luna*
Baldassare Galuppi

Respiration and Support
Practice panting to learn flexible and buoyant breathing, which is needed throughout this aria. Panting will help to teach the catch breath.

Practice this exercise on various beats on spoken then sung pitch:
1st time spoken [i], 2nd time sung [i].

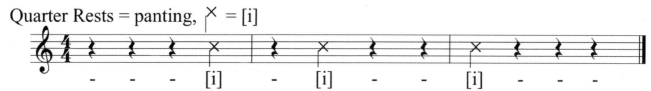

Reset the breath, then try this pattern.

Resonance
Practice scales on various vowel combinations. We have included examples, but also make up your own exercises, and be sure to mix it up! Finally, apply these exercises to the scales found in the song.

Phonation

Mimicking the melodic idea, practice these ascending and descending figures. The technique found in the exercises can then be carried into the aria.

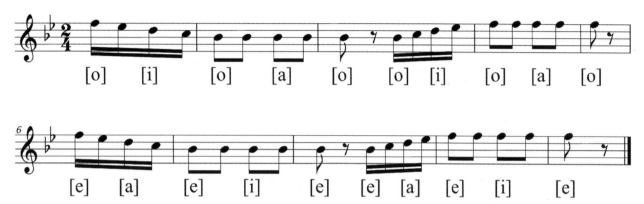

Registration

Lower *passaggio*:

Extract *sono così* for lower *passaggio* scale work on closed vowels. Precede the descending intervals with an elongated "sss" to ensure movement of the breath.

Lower *passaggio*:

Take advantage of the double consonants in words like *lilla, fuggi,* and *fatta* for lower *passaggio* coordination.

Upper *passaggio*:

The rhythm in this section will help upper *passaggio* registration issues, releasing tension from the vocal tract. Practice on various vowels.

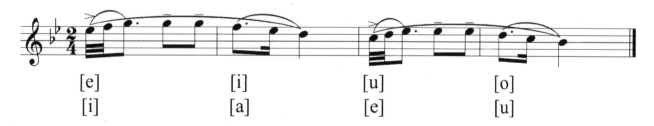

Diction/Articulation

Intone text from this aria on spoken pitch, moving smoothly and slowly from syllable to syllable. To maintain stability of the larynx, practice intoning these phrases with legato and stabilized articulation.
For example:

"Quuuaaandooo sssiii trooovvvaaanooo"
"leee baaasseee fffeeemmiiineee"

Phonetic Transcription and Translation of the Text

Quando   si   trovano
[ˈkwan.do si   tro.ˈvaː.no]
When one meets

le   basse   femmine,
[le   ˈbas.se   ˈfem.mi.ne]
those crude women,

dicono,   parlano
[ˈdiː.ko.no   par.ˈlaː.no]
they speak, they talk

spesso   così.
[ˈspes.so   ko.ˈziː]
like that all the time.

Eh,   non   sapete?
[eːɪ   non   sa.ˈpeː.te]
"Hey, haven't you heard

Nina   l'ha   fatta!
[ˈniː.na   la   ˈfat.ta]
what Nina did?

Eh,   cosa   dite?
[eːɪ   ˈkɔː.za   ˈdiː.te]
"What did you say?"

"Lilla   fuggì".
[ˈlil.la   ˈfud.dʒi]
"Lilla ran off"

le   basse   femmine,
[le   ˈbas.se   ˈfem.mi.ne]
those crude women,

Quando si trovano…

Le   triste   femmine
[le   ˈtri.ste   fem.ˈmiː.ne]
Those unfortunate women

sono   così.
[ˈsoː.no   co.ˈziː]
I'm just like them.

Quando si trovano le basse femmine

from *Il mondo della luna*

Carlo Goldoni

Baldassarre Galuppi
(1706-1785)

Allegro Moderato ♩ = 96

Lisetta

Quan - do_ si tro - va-no, le bas-se_ fem - mi-ne di-co-no,

so - no co - sì. Quan-do si tro-va-no, di-co-no, par-la-no:

Eh, non sa - pe- te? Eh, co-sa di-te? Le___ bas-se fem-mi-ne,

le___ bas-se fem-mi-ne so - no, so - no, so - no co-

so - no__ co - sì, so - no co - sì, so - no co - sì.

Chi mi vuol bene presto me dica

Aria from *La Finta Semplice*
Wolfgang Amadeus Mozart

Respiration and Support

Practice exercises that require agility and wide-ranging intervals to develop skills of respiration and support for this aria. Be creative!

1. [e]
2. [i]

Resonance

The vowel [i] appears many times in the text of this aria. The following exercise is intended to develop a resonant core by moving from [i] to [a], [i] to [o], and [i] to [u], and then reversing [a] to [i], [o] to [i] and [u] to [i].

[i]   [i   -   a]   [a   -   i]

1. [i]
2. [i   -   o   -   ]
3. [o   -   i   -   ]

1. [i]
2. [i   -   u   -   ]
3. [u   -   i   -   ]

Phonation

This aria provides an opportunity to maintain vibrancy through rests. Practice singing through the rests, as shown below.

Registration

The ascending figures in the melody help to maintain a connection to a resonant core of sound. Keep the connection to the open throat of the lower pitches while ascending.

Diction/Articulation

Referring to the resonance exercise, shift focus to the movement of the tongue from one vowel to the next. Efficient articulation requires that the transitions from vowel to vowel be fluid. Any tongue tension will prevent legato or lyric articulation.

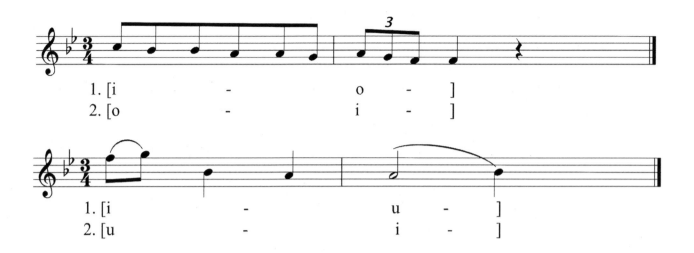

1. [i - o -]
2. [o - i -]

1. [i - u -]
2. [u - i -]

Phonetic Transcription and Translation of Text

Chi mi voul   bene,
[ki   mi   vwɔːl   ˈbɛː.ne]
Whoever loves me,

presto   mel   dica,
[ˈprɛ.sto   mel   ˈdiː.ka]
should tell me right away,

che   per   capire
[ke   per   ka.ˈpiː.ɾe]
Because to understand

non   vo'   fatica,
[non   vɔ   fa.ˈtiː.ka]
I don't want to make an effort

nè   intisichire
[nɛ   in.ti.si.ˈkiː.ɾe]
nor languish

per   civiltà.
[per   tʃi.vil.ˈtaː]
out of propriety.

Tutti i biglietti
[ˈtut.‿ti   biʎ.ˈʎet.ti]
All of the notes

io   ve   li   dono:
[iːo   ve   li   ˈdoː.no]
I give them to you:

sono   seccaggini,
[ˈso.no   sek.ˈkad.d͡ʒini]
they're bothersome

son   melensaggini
[son   mɛ.lɛn.ˈsad.d͡ʒi.ni]
they're nonsense,

e   alla   più   presta
[e   ˈal.la   pju   ˈprɛ.sta]
and it's the simplest

da   testa   a   testa
[da   ˈtɛs.ta   a   ˈtɛs.ta]
when face to face

tutto   si   fa
[ˈtut.to   si   fa]
all is done.

Page intentionally left blank to facilitate page turns

Chi mi vuol bene presto mel dica

from *La Finta Semplice*

Marco Coltellini

W.A. Mozart
(1756-1791)

per ci - vil - tà, nè in-ti-si - chi-re per ci-vil - tà,

per ci - vil - tá, nè in ti - si - chi - re per ci - vil - tà.

Tut-ti i bi -

glietti io ve li dono, so-no sec-cag-gi-ni,

son me-lan-sag-gi-ni e al-la più pre-sta da te-sta a te-sta

tut-to si fà e al-la più pre-sta da te-sta a

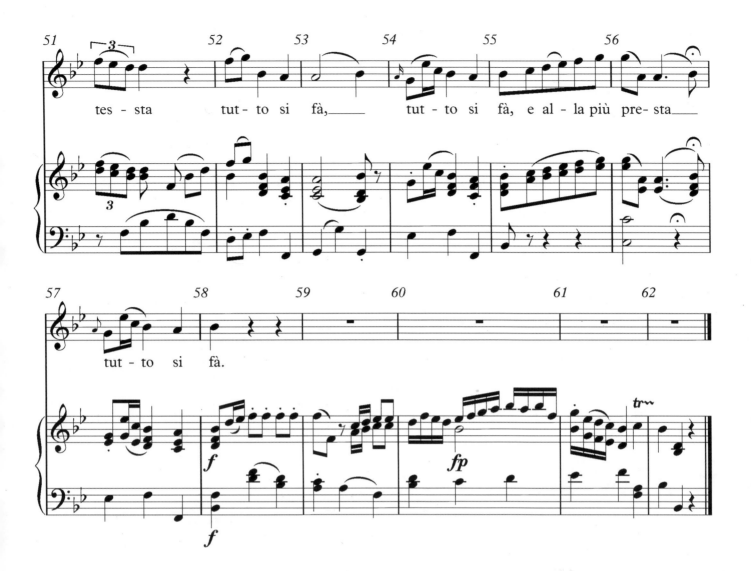

tes - sta   tut - to si   fà,_____   tut - to si   fà, e al - la più pre - sta_____

tut - to si   fà.

Sample Rubric for Grading Repertoire

Scale of 1-5
0-20 points easy, 20-40 points moderate, 40-60 points difficult

Technical Issue Addressed	Problem Solving Questions	Scale 1-5
ACCOMPANIMENT	Is the accompaniment utilitarian, supportive, independent, etc.? Is the accompaniment part of the story line? Descriptive e.g. water figures, spinning wheel, etc.?	
CHARACTERIZATION/ACTING	Is the character appropriate to the student's dramatic capacity or life experiences? Will the student benefit from portraying this type of character?	
DICTION/ARTICULATION	Consideration of challenging consonant clusters. Closed position or difficult consonants on challenging pitches? Student's knowledge of French, Italian, Russian, German, etc. language or diction?	
DYNAMICS	Is the singer expected to sing a pianissimo high note? Are the markings pedagogically helpful (e.g. crescendo on sustained notes to assist in breath energy and/or vibrancy?)	
MELISMATIC PHRASES	Beginner or advanced melismas/melismatic phrases present? Appoggiatura? Dotted rhythms?	
MUSICAL CONSIDERATIONS	Through composed? Strophic? Accessible harmonic language? Tonal? An enjoyable melody?	
RANGE/TESSITURA	How are high notes approached—dramatically? Is the range too vast? Is the tessitura too low or high? Can a young singer sit in that particular part of the voice for that long without fatiguing?	
REGISTRATION	Does the piece assist in working through *passaggio* issues? Will the student carry weight up? Helpful vowels in an underdeveloped part of the student's voice? Etc.	
RESPIRATION	Are phrase lengths accessible? Will the breaths allow for renewal of positioning?	
TEXT SETTING	Syllabic, Patter Song, Lyric? Does the text setting assist in memorization?	
VOWELS/VOWEL SEQUENCES	Observation of vowels in *passaggio*. Will vowel patterns assist in correcting vocal faults forward to back, tongue position, etc.?	
WORDS: POETRY/LYRICS/LIBRETTO	Is this accessible poetry? Is the story age appropriate? Will the text make the memorization process difficult?	